beatitude

New & Selected Poems

beatitude

New & Selected Poems

For

Pat Rink

John R. McDonough

ISBN-13: 978-1719321167
Library of Congress Control Number: 2018906441

Printed in the United States of America

DEDICATION

To my brothers
Jim
George (dec.)
Dismas (dec.)
Gaylan
John P.

And to the Men's Prayer Group
St. Patrick Catholic Church and School
Tacoma, Washington
Brothers All

Special thanks to Gavin MacHutchin
for the front cover art work
And to Jimmy McDonough for the back cover photograph

Veritas - Gaudium - Pacem

TABLE OF CONTENTS

beatitude / be(attitude)

Nature's Miracles

The Search

The Good Life

Sacraments

LIST OF PHOTOGRAPHS

FOREWORD

John McDonough has given his readers another gift in this volume of poems—or, rather, many gifts, as each utterance is its own gift.

Most of the poems are new here, though some were part of his earlier collections. His reflection on the joy of summer in "Summer Solstice," for example, with its wonderful concluding image of "A long parabola toward winter's sting" first appeared in *The Open Door*. They are included again here because they touch on the theme of beatitudes, and blessings.

And this collection is John's blessing on us.

Designers have always insisted that form must follow function. But we often imagine that *artists* are not bound by such petty concerns. Many people see the artist as a person who would never allow himself to be confined by formal strictures or limitations.

And yet John McDonough has embraced formal poetry in this collection. The reader will notice that these are *all* formal poems: most are sonnets, several others are villanelles, and a few are built from rhymed couplets. And, thus, they all have rules.

But I suspect McDonough wouldn't have it any other way. The form of these poems follows from their function.

McDonough sees liberation in choosing to commit to something outside the Self. Within these formal structures, he finds interesting language when working with the rules of rhythm and rhyme, language which illuminates ideas that might not otherwise have been discovered if he hadn't needed to search his prodigious vocabulary for a word that *fits*—which is the message that many of these poems have for all of us. Surrender, and you will find it's not surrender at all, but freedom. Throughout this collection, there is the theme of *choosing* to follow the Word of God, and McDonough underscores that message in his own choice of formal poetry.

McDonough himself explains the ingenious layout of the first part of this volume, with its conversation between pairs of sonnets—one sonnet exemplifying the beatitudes and another resisting their message—and punctuated by a pair of villanelles at the end.

This is a brave approach, since it offers "equal time" to both points of view, and McDonough is convincing when inhabiting these other voices. In his counterpoint to meekness, the speaker says, "I am not now, nor ever will be meek,/The meek are losers" in a voice that believes what it says.

McDonough is not offering us easy answers here. Note how many of the poems begin by posing questions. For instance, in his reflection on the blessing of those "who hunger and thirst for righteousness," McDonough asks *six* questions. And even when it might feel like an answer, the answer is often a version of "only God knows."

And in addition to calling upon his understanding of poetic forms, McDonough mines his knowledge of Aquinas and Aristotle in "The Good Life," of architecture and anatomy in "Fortitude." His poem "Time"—which first appeared in *Casting About*—makes playful use of astronomy and enumerates the various ways the planets play havoc with "sleep and birthdays." And in other poems, he muses on tides, chemistry, and more—not least among them, religion and interpersonal relationships.

It has been nearly three years since McDonough's last collection of poems. And at the time he told those close to him that he had written all the poems he had in him. He should have known better. And we are blessed for it not having been so.

Gary Mesick
March 2018

EDITOR'S PREFACE

It has always been a pleasure to read and review the poetic works of John R. McDonough. I have done so in the past, meeting with him on numerous occasions to help edit and organize his poems into chapter sections. These meetings have occurred at each other's homes, our spouses present, all four of us actively engaged in the literary design and book-building conversations. There would be food and beverages on the table and gaiety in the air, a prevailing lightness of heart, but also a let's get down to business incentive, each of us knowing that this was another golden opportunity to assist John in a poetic creation. This latest book, *beatitude*, marks his fourth book of published poems since 2013. Dr. John has proven to be a prolific writer, a person of rare insight and intelligence, an inspired art-ist with a deep well of words and ideas and perceptions. Once again, it has been an honor to share in his literary endeavors.

There are five separate sections in this book. Each rep-resents a general theme and literary intent. There are new poems (never published before) and selected poems chosen from his three previous books of poetry (*Casting About, The Open Door, Winter Sun*). Blended together, the poems show-case a galvanizing core of subjects ranging from the mir-acles of nature to the search and components of a good life to the spiritual notions of the sacraments. The opening section, "beatitude" (the title of the book) refers to the di-vine in all of us – our inherent capacity for goodness and love and fellowship. However, you will find juxtaposed opposite each "beatitude" poem a verse entitled "be(attitude)"which casts shadows upon our weaknesses and deficiencies. Dr. John provides a provocative view of the human dilemma (one I will read again and again and remember for a long while) - the ongoing struggle of the sacred and the profane, of hope over despair, of enduring faith and charity and kindness in a world sometimes gone far, far astray.

Enjoy the poems, I say. Relish in Dr. John's choice of words. Find a comfortable chair and a quiet uninterrupted hour or more and ponder the greater ideals and the important messages spoken in his verses. This is what I have done and I have been ever so justly rewarded.

Joseph Galagan
May 20, 2018

ACKNOWLEDGMENTS

It has been seven years since the Galagans, Joe and Katherine, and Gary Mesick began assisted me in the editing, and formatting of six published works. The present book of poems, *beatitude*, joins three other books of poetry: *Casting About* (2013), *The Open Door* (2014), and *Winter Sun* (2015). To these were added two of prose: *The Good Doctor* (2016), and *Angels and Other Stories* (2017).

Gary, Joe and Katherine are remarkable persons. I would be remiss should I neglect to cite their participation, some items of background and their expertise. This journey into serious writing and publishing has forged enduring friendships.

Gary and I first met several years ago after Sunday mass. We were conversing with another parishioner who complained bitterly about the terrible state of world affairs. I then quipped: "God's in His heaven, all's right with the world, Shakespeare". Then came a voice: "Browning". It was Gary. In an emphatic, yet not overbearing way, he had supplied the correct author. I later learned that Gary had graduated from the U.S. Military Academy at West Point, followed by a Doctorate in English Literature from Harvard University, and then returned to the Academy where he taught English Literature. Gary has reviewed my writing before publication, and supplied a Foreword for this book as well as my second book of poetry, *The Open Door*.

The Galagans are both authors. Joe has written several books, especially a poignant memoir about his bout with acute leukemia as a high school student. Joe has two Master of Arts degrees - one from Syracuse University in Counseling, and the other from University College, Dublin, in Irish Literature. Joe has served as editor for all of my books. Katherine, Joe's wife, has a Doctor of Medicine degree from the University of Washington, and advanced residency training in Pathology from Syracuse University, and the University of Washington. Katherine is an eminent pathologist and has co-authored and edited several color atlases for the College of American Pathologists, as well as an art book called *The Healing Art of Pathology*. She has formatted all of my books.

To Gary, Joe and Katherine go my unending gratitude.

JRM

INTRODUCTION

Beatitudes are those divinely-inspired sayings by Jesus that lay out a way of living; a pattern for the way lives should be lived; a set of directives for leading the GOOD life. Beatitude means blessing - divinely inspired, they have a power that applies to Christian believers, but also to non-believers, those of other faiths, and those with no faith at all.

There is an enigmatic passage from the Gospel of John that may speak to this:

> *I am the Good Shepherd and I know mine and mine know Me. I have other sheep that do not belong to this fold. These also I must lead, and they will hear My voice, and there will be one flock, one shepherd. (John 10:14-17) No one can take them out of My hand. My Father who has given them to Me is greater than all, and no one can take them out of My Father's hand. My Father and I are one. (John 10:28-30)*

I've used the sonnet, a poem of fourteen lines, to illustrate each of the eight beatitudes. English and Italian (Petrarchan) sonnets are interchanged, and a final, ninth summarization is presented as a villanelle, a nineteen-line poem, similar to a Sonnet.

Both types of sonnets and the villanelle are centuries old, and require strict rules such as iambic line form, and rhyme sequences. In addition, the villanelle requires recurring refrains, also in a strict format.

To illustrate the "reach" of beatitude for believer and non-believer, each beatitude is presented on facing pages, titled as "beatitude" for believers, and "(be)attitude" for non-believers. To further illustrate the "connectedness" between "beatitude" and "(be)attitude", the author has introduced another element. The rhyming word at the end of each line is identical for the two sets. This applies to both the sonnets and the villanelles.

Other poems are introduced where blessing may augment daily life such as virtue, sacrament, and the glories of creation. In addition to sonnets and villanelles, the reader will encounter an occasional ode. Selected poems, when they bespeak blessing, have also been included from prior published poetry by the author: *Casting About, 100 Lyric Poems from the Heart* (2013), *The Open Door* (2014), and *Winter Sun* (2015).

beatitude
be(attitude)

beatitude

blessed are the poor in spirit

I am, and thus I know that I am poor.
 I did not choose to be, I only came,
From You my God and parents such grandeur,
 From nothing to a person with a name.

Mind and will reflect on every thing,
 Nature's glory, life's unbending road.
Life so short, what do our efforts bring?
 And what remains, when gone, are payments owed?

You said I Am. You are the source of all.
 Though poor You helped me to a future still.
I am a creature burdensome and small,
 Yet loved by You to share Your Divine Will.

What lies in store, eternal bliss we know,
And poor ones drawn by You will be aglow.

be(attitude)

blessed are the poor in spirit

> I am rich, and I will shun the poor.
> The rich get richer this is whence I came,
> I stand atop my tower such grandeur,
> I am a person branded with my name.
>
> I move at will and possess every thing,
> I travel where I want on any road,
> I am important, others to me bring,
> Their pleas for mercy, I take what is owed.
>
> And God? I will not think of You at all,
> You cannot help, I have my future still.
> I know myself, magnificent not small,
> I am too occupied to heed Your will.
>
> What lies in store? That is for fools to know.
> Why beckon me? My life is all aglow.

beatitude

blessed are they who mourn

I mourn when parent or a loved one dies.
  Beyond the flow of tears a deep crevasse.
Sorrow if to choose I would bypass,
  And forge a mood of solace, a disguise.
But tears well up to fill unblinking eyes,
  And fall to moisten trodden flattened grass,
As memories filter through then slowly pass,
  While crypt accepts the buried as it's prize.

But what should we retain of this sad day?
  The cemetery holds our loved one dear.
But body only what of heart and soul?
  That precious spirit heaven bound we pray.
Released from mortal bondage free we cheer,
  No sorrow needed when the bell does toll.

be(attitude)

blessed are they who mourn

I do not waste my time when someone dies.
  For family such may leave a deep crevasse.
Sorrow not my way, I will bypass.
  Crocodile tears a tawdry feigned disguise.
I do detest those fools with teary eyes,
  Splashing wanton tears upon the grass.
I watch while carrying they slowly pass,
  Then drop into the opened earth their prize.

What can be drawn from this a dreary day?
  The sorrowing have placed a loved one dear,
They then whine on and ask, but what of soul?
  They think it's heaven bound, for this they pray.
What fools! Now free of you, for this I'll cheer.
  I'll not think of when the bell does toll.

beatitude

blessed are the meek

Why should there be a blessing for the meek?
  Does this portend no blessing for the strong?
Might this imply the meek are also weak?
  Or do I have the formulation wrong?

Humility an attitude bestowed
  By Jesus as He lived His mortal life.
Obedient to His Father, death He owed
  His meekness strength against impending strife.

If we want to live as Jesus bade,
  Then meekness must be central to our way.
Grace and goodness fill our souls arrayed,
  With strength beyond our knowing if we pray.

The doorway to our souls is opened wide.
Humility the key if we abide.

be(attitude)

blessed are the meek

I am not now, nor ever will be meek.
　The meek are losers, I myself am strong,
I take what's mine, and more. The meek are weak.
　Don't waste my time to ask if this is wrong.

Humility some feel is theirs bestowed.
　They pander this is how to lead your life.
For me, I'll not be bound, I've nothing owed.
　The humble set themselves for future strife.

Some would say this is what Jesus bade.
　But this is for the weak, the loser's way.
Fame my choice, is how I am arrayed.
　I will not waste my life with those who pray.

The doorway to my world I open wide,
Enjoyment is the key, this I abide.

beatitude

blessed are they who hunger and thirst for righteousness

Right from wrong is that what we're about?
  Can we decipher what is meant by that?
And should the effort be a true combat?
  And if we lose a baleful forlorn shout?
And what of thirst and hunger, what of doubt?
  Our need for sustenance is where we're at.
We satisfy our body's need for fat,
  But are we meant to seek a different route?

I am the Way the Truth the Light the Life.
  Learn from Me and follow to be saved.
And to be saved is to be free at last,
  Free of other paths that lead to strife.
Let your heart be holy, thus engraved,
And righteousness your treasure to hold fast.

be(attitude)

blessed are they who hunger and thirst for righteousness

Righteousness, that's not what I'm about.
  Might makes right, what do you think of that?
I punch and counterpunch my true combat,
  And I put down the weak ones with a shout.
When vanquished they are left without a doubt,
  The strong will win, and that is where I'm at.
I take, then take some more, take all the fat,
  Only dummies seek a righteous route.

Mine the way, I bend the truth, that's life.
  I put away, some money to be saved,
The rest I spend, won't have to make it last.
  So what! I take what leads to other's strife,
It's what I'm famous for, my name's engraved.
Righteousness is foolish to hold fast.

beatitude

blessed are the merciful

Mercy and power a strange dichotomy.
  The one a source of good the other force.
The beggar pleads a piece of bread from thee,
  The rich one says begone you block my course.

Mercy thus a choice, to give or not,
  And giving, mercy needs no recompense.
Mercy given thus of love begot,
  Entwined beneficence lets good commence.

God of love and mercy, power freed.
  Engulfs the world wherein we do all dwell.
God's Son upon a cross in pain to bleed,
  To vanquish sin and and thus to save from hell.

Men of mercy conform to God the Just.
God's own image and likeness thereby thrust.

be(attitude)

blessed are the merciful

Mercy and love a strange dichotomy,
   I love myself, and power is my force.
If in my way, my wrath I place on thee,
   I will not ever let you block my course.

Mercy, pshaw! For fools! For me it's not.
   Those that use it get no recompense.
And what of those that mercy has begot?
   They have no mainstay, gain cannot commence.

Rid your mind of mercy, thus be freed.
   Use power on this earth whereon we dwell.
Strength the proper course, the weak will bleed.
   I care not for their ever living hell.

Might makes right, I care not for the just,
Power is god for those on whom it's thrust.

beatitude

blessed are the clean of heart

Do not look back at outward man that way.
　While outer garments show a perfect fit,
The washed and groomed for formal portraits sit,
　But underneath the heart and soul hold sway.
To find the clean of heart discard array.
　Instead look deep within and then admit,
A sweet aroma do such souls emit,
　Of honor, truth and goodness God's bouquet.

An unclean heart is chained in filth, unfree.
　Ever chasing shadows found unreal.
Longing for that water a soul to clean.
　Deep unhappiness a wayward plea.
Oh God I know You can, please help me heal,
　And to my heart restore its prior sheen.

be(attitude)

blessed are the clean of heart

I do not cater to this saintly way,
  A category that I will not fit,
Nor will I in such presence ever sit.
  Desire I will use, others to sway,
To satisfy my longing in array,
  And overpower women who admit,
Molestation, evil, I emit?
  Accusations! Groundless, vain bouquet.

Chastity, a heart that is unfree,
  A sterile life, so servile and unreal,
Forsaking lust, pretending to be clean.
  My choice is forage. While my victims plea,
My libido expands and will not heal,
  Nor ever give me back my prior sheen.

beatitude

blessed are the peacemakers

> Beware the call at night or early morn,
>   From house conflicted, two or more in strife.
> The sergeant tells his class, all rookies sworn,
>   Your life may be at risk from gun or knife.
>
> Peacemaking a risky, iffy flair.
>   What are the skills that usher in success?
> Fairness, patient listening, brings new care,
>   When both sides trust, they both are wont to bless.
>
> Peacemaking a noble trait to bring.
>   Risk without reward the watchword here.
> Patience, hard work, prayer, to this we cling,
>   Let evanescent peace not disappear.
>
> Let honor, truth, and goodness have their sway.
> Then solace to both parties has a way.

be(attitude)

blessed are the peacemakers

> Peace is thrust at me from early morn,
>   From fearful ones who are afraid of strife.
> But conflict is my path, to this I'm sworn,
>   I will, if need be, use the gun or knife.
>
> Peacemaking, a useless iffy flair,
>   History shows it is without success.
> A waste of time, be sure that I don't care,
>   And have no room for those who wish to bless.
>
> Antagonize! It's what I wish to bring,
>   Turmoil is my sport, my watchword here.
> My gain your loss, to this I'll ever cling,
>   The jungle rules, and peace will disappear.
>
> I'll use whatever ruses have their sway,
> When honor, truth or goodness not the way.

beatitude

blessed are they who are persecuted for the sake of
righteousness

> Persecution's dread conundrum here.
>   Why do faithful have this as a fate?
> Why stand, then be exposed to murderous hate?
>   When loftier goals are those that we endear.
> Might not we turn and run when danger near?
>   And hide from harm until the risks abate?
> This surely is our right, not our debate,
>   But caught, then charges brought, provoking fear.
>
> Our Savior freely died in love for us
>   Love is thus the point of suffering.
> We show our love for God by standing firm
>   Then pray for strength to stay and triumph, thus:
> Suffering, even death, our offering.
>   Our faith, our hope, our love we thus affirm.

be(attitude)

blessed are they who are persecuted for the sake of righteousness

> The persecuted have no bearing here.
>   Unlucky ones, that is their foresworn fate.
> The persecutors, we, are theirs to hate,
>   While they stand for ideals they endear.
> Rightness, wrongness, I keep neither near,
>   May animus towards me at once abate,
> Then not become a source of foul debate.
>   Now there is nothing that I have to fear.
>
> They say their Jesus died in love for us.
>   Is love the central point of suffering?
> Resolute they stand so stout and firm,
>   Their message resonates, a triumph thus?
> They suffer, even die, an offering?
>   Of faith, of hope, of love, they thus affirm.

beatitude

blessed are you when they insult you and persecute you
and utter every kind of evil against you falsely because
of Me

> We live with God for all eternity.
>   If here on earth we practice every day,
> And love with all our hearts His just decree.
>
> Be poor in spirit true humility,
>   Seek mercy for all others, fears allay,
> We live with God for all eternity.
>
> We mourn those members of the human tree,
>   When difficulties mount and come their way,
> And love with all our hearts His just decree.
>
> Let us make peace to set the shackled free,
>   To usher in new hope for former prey,
> We live with God for all eternity.
>
> From all uncleanliness our hearts should flee,
>   And yet from persecution never stray,
> And love with all our hearts His just decree.
>
> Hunger and thirst our souls' tranquility,
>   For righteousness to ever keep in play.
> We live with God for all eternity.
>   And love with all our hearts His just decree.

be(attitude)

blessed are you when they insult you and persecute you
and utter every kind of evil against you falsely because
of Me

But now I wonder of eternity.
  What if I do not have another day?
What might await, if such His just decree?

And poor in spirit? Why humility?
  And mercy? Fears that we should e'er allay?
But now I wonder of eternity.

Why mourn those members of the human tree,
  When difficulties mount and come their way?
What might await, if such His just decree?

They say make peace and set the shackled free,
  The lowly ones whom I have used as prey.
But now I wonder of eternity.

I have an unclean heart. How should I flee?
  And yet from justice I can never stray.
What might await, if such His just decree?

Will thirst of soul restore tranquility?
  Can righteousness be ever kept in play?
But now I wonder of eternity.
  What might await, if such His just decree?

Nature's Miracles

Sky

Spacious firmament, the air, thy sea,
　Engulfs the earth in endless custody.
The wind in ceaseless torrents sweeps across,
　Vast stretches of our world with wanton ease.

Meteor showers seek to penetrate,
　And pocket earth with havoc far and wide,
But air incinerates these roguish rocks,
　All harmless, except for those of giant size.

Ocean air embraces tumbling wave,
　And like a kiss, the ocean yields its gift.
Pure water, without salt, in plenitude,
　To drench dry fields and mountains far away.

Dioxide of carbon plant must have,
　To build its structure, oxygen released.
And air, that mighty engine of exchange,
　Sustains the life of animal and man.

(from *Casting About,* p. 3)

The Tree

Once I heard a tree that spoke to me.
  Not words, but sounds, a rustic symphony.
Buds that sprang in spring from wintery freeze,
  To start the leaves a fluttering in the breeze.
The leaves grew out, they spoke again to me,
  As swirling winds brought new intensity,
And louder sounds, as twigs and branches sway,
  The swishing sounds renew symphonic play.

Summer storms cause havoc to the tree.
  The branches bend, some crack, disharmony.
Then gentle rain, a pelting tambour beat,
  Restore symphonic semblance, quenching treat.
Autumn brings new color, leaves grow old.
  October winds add crackle in the cold.
November storms are here, leaves flutter down,
  Orchestral strings, while settling to the ground.

The next sounds harsh, the leaves raked to a pyre.
  The rake now used to scoop them to the fire,
Bright flames, blue smoke, all swirling in the mash,
  And pungent smell, then all that's left is ash.
Hibernate in winter, nature said.
  The symphony not dead, only delayed.
The old tree sleeps, will speak in time its ring,
  But you must wait, be patient for the spring.

The family, like a tree, with many cares,
  Sometimes symphonic, lovely tonal airs.
But when discordant, dreadful sounds to hear,
  Like cracking of the branches, hard to bear.
But trees have roots, and so do families.
  Roots that strengthen, nourish, and sustain,
And seasons that unfold, all kinds of change,
  As members grow, and go their merry ways.

Some, like leaves, uncertain destinies.
Others, seeds, the start of family trees.

(from *Casting About*, p. 6)

The River

Water moving downward to the sea,
  Ever changing in its vibrant swirl.
Floating leaves and twigs of trees flow free,
  While rocks form eddy currents all awhirl.

Translucent swatch shows crawly things below
  For trout to grab, a meal on the fly.
Water ouzels dive into the flow,
  They swim, then climb on mossy rock to dry.

Fast water tumbles over barrier rocks,
  Long stretches with white mists above the surge,
Until a gentler slope its rush unlocks,
  To deeper pools, the roiling waters merge.

Otters frolic on the bank, their way,
Then waters slip into the briny bay.

(from *The Open Door*, p. 3)

Summer Solstice

The summer solstice came to us today.
  We saw the sun, and billowing cumulous cloud.
Despite the sunshine, heat has been astray,
  Solstice heat not in our northern shroud.

The tide was very low, a minus four,
  The sun is nearer earth this time of year.
Moon is closer too, in full galore.
  Both contribute to our tidal fare.

Wife Jane and I sat on our patio,
  Pleasant idle small talk our delight.
A hummingbird seen in its feeding glow,
  Brilliant green, with wings a blurry sight.

Tomorrow's day begins its shortened ring,
A long parabola toward winter's sting.

(from *The Open Door*, p. 6)

Our World

What is there not to love in this our world
  We inhabit, free, at will to roam.
Our needs are satisfied, we are encircled,
  But always find a way to come back home.

The earth, this great abode, gives all we need,
  Food and shelter, wraps to keep out cold,
And others like ourselves to plant our seed,
  The generations posit what we hold.

Good abounds in what we see around,
  But evil too, gets in the way of this.
We know the difference, can put evil down,
  And live life to the full in earthly bliss.

We need not be the victim, evil's thrall,
Love all but evil, that can be our call.

(from *Winter Sun*, p. 32)

By Degrees

Warmth we feel within a narrow range,
  Seventy to eighty Fahrenheit degrees, let's say,
(We vary individually, not so strange),
  But narrow we want the comfort zone to stay.

At the upper end, the heat goes far,
  Millions of degrees, no end in sight,
Exposed, our earth, and all contained, would char,
  Then turn to clouds of heated gas and light.

We're closer at the low end of the line,
  To absolute zero, removal of all heat.
In fahrenheit minus four hundred fifty-nine,
  All motion stops, no heart can beat.

Was Dante* serendipitous to place
Satan blocked in ice, impervious to grace?

*Dante Alighieri (1265-1321)
The Divine Comedy.

(from *Winter Sun*, p. 16)

Winter Sun

It's cold outside.
  But here behind this window facing south,
Sunshine floods the room.

Like a warm blanket enfolding all in sight.
  Rays through window's sheen enhance
Floating particles in a sparkling dance
  Wafting free, spectacular display,
Then gone again beyond the sunlight's glint,
  While others swarm within and glisten bright.

Clouds form and darken this our winter's sun.
  Vanishing rays, the glitter of particles gone.
Sunshine's warming bath slow ebbs away.
  Await the winter sun another day.

(from *Winter Sun*, p. 3)

Nature's Miracles

Things that make us wonder, they abound.
  Abundant growth, we see it every day.
Animals and plants they're all around.
  From embryo or seed, they have their way.

We know a lot about what makes things grow,
  They're everywhere, we pay them little heed,
But still, mysterious things we do not know,
  While science marches to discovery's creed.

Six carbon atoms chained, the basis for
  Our carbohydrate food. Or bound in sixes,
The wood of trees for building shelves, or more.
  Nature's way, simplicity with fixes.

If science could learn all there is, we'd know
Miracles spill from God's abundant flow.

(from *Winter Sun*, p. 11)

Starlight

Stars, the light source in the universe.
  Other heavenly bodies reflect light.
Uncounted trillions, stars their lights disperse.

Our sun, one minor star, earth's light to nurse,
  Daytime warming's presence blazing bright,
Stars, the light source in the universe.

Night or day, earth's rotor does coerce,
  Variance gifted only to our sight.
Uncounted trillions, stars their lights disperse.

These stars at night pinpoints of light immerse
  Our senses as we gaze in awed delight.
Stars, the light source in the universe.

Wherefore the margins that these stars traverse?
  The universe, unfathomed at its site,
Uncounted trillions, stars their lights disperse.

Stars, emergent light from God's own purse,
  Sparkle in the caverns of the night.
Stars, the light source in the universe.
  Uncounted trillions, stars their lights disperse.

(from *The Open Door*, p. 104)

Motion

Motion becomes us.
  Creatures near and far,
Rapid as the falcon,
  Or cheetah on the run,
Others slow,
  As redwood's growing rings.

For creatures, motion comes,
  For need for food to eat,
Or nighttime settled sleep,
  Or shade from daytime heat,
Or yen from deep within,
  For others when in need.

Hills and valleys,
  Plains and streams,
In motion too, though not innate,
  Gravity, tectonic plates,
Produce a shifting place to place,
  All in motion just the same.

(from *The Open Door*, p. 11)

Clouds

Water droplets in the sky,
Coalesce in varied form.
Stratus, nimbus, cumulus,
With cirrus a kaleidoscope
Of textures, shapes, and colors.
What glorious globs of firmament
The clouds.
Infinitely changeable, and yet,
Unchanging in their life-dependent task
Of layering the earth one meter deep
Each year with water.

(from *Casting About*, p. 8)

Connected

Little things will sometimes give a clue
  Of what we're made of, some surprises too.
Oxy - hydro - nitro, these three guns,
  Plus carbon make up ninety six percent
Of human body mass, just think of that.

Elements that unaffected issue
  For brief sojourns within our body's tissue.
They come and go as part of nature's climes,
  Unchanged from where they were in bygone times,
The same as they will be for ages still.

In this regard, we're made of stuff that brings
  The ancient fabric of all living things.
Ancestors, toads, and toadstools, all do spare,
  Their elements for all of life to share,
We are connected to all living things.

(from *Casting About*, p. 73)

Inner Space

If we could see the stuff of which we're made,
   Protons, neutrons, electrons all awhirl,
Tiny particles, a cavalcade,
   Dancing in their awesome rhythmic twirl.

Molecular structures all are interlaced,
   Making up our torso, arms, and face,
Inner organs too, and all are placed,
   Within a skin, an outer holding case.

These molecules that form our inmost stuff,
   Are mostly space, a void with nothing there,
If all the matter were compressed enough,
   A golf ball size remains, the weight to bear.

Space, a thousand times the solid fill
Our structure, a marvelous making of God's will.

(from *Casting About*, p. 74)

Moonlight

Dazzling light on water strewn.
  Sitting on the beach in awe,
We saw this glorious moon

This wondrous orb, enchanting boon,
  Worthy of our last hurrah,
Dazzling light on water strewn.

Poems and songs we fondly croon,
  They poorly ape like yellow straw.
We saw this glorious moon.

How lovely was this night in June,
  Artists can't in justice draw,
Dazzling light on water strewn.

We sat enraptured on the dune,
  Vast beauty with no evident flaw,
We saw this glorious moon.

Radiance enough to make one swoon,
  And dance after long winter's thaw,
Dazzling light on water strewn.
  We saw this glorious moon.

(from *The Open Door*, p. 10)

The Rose

A pristine morning, dew upon the grass.
  A thorny stem bends rising toward the sky.
A bud is seen, not yet in bloom alas,
  The future flower evokes a saddened sigh.

Yet adjacent, another thorny stem,
  Is topped by opened flower, dewy rose,
Shimmering petals, translucent lovely gem,
  Soft pink layers, beauty nature chose.

Perfuming air, unmatched by any thing,
  Nature can produce in myriad ways.
Flower atop the thorn, a painful sting,
  While holding thorny stem, its top ablaze.

If heaven holds the power to decor,
The beauty of the rose, what lies in store?

(from *The Open Door,* p. 4)

Leaves

Leaves are forming now in early spring.
  Flattened structures pointing to the light.
Their stems are fastened to the twigs of trees.
  Fluttering in the breeze, their greens so bright.

They breath like us, but in a different way,
  Dioxide of carbon they absorb,
Then oxygen exudes to sky away,
  Everywhere around our earthly orb.

These little leaves, a part of God's creation.
  So tiny, yet so vital to augment,
The atmosphere, maintaining concentration,
  Of oxygen at twenty-point-nine percent.

Animals and humans breath so free,
Dependent on the leaves upon a tree.

(from *Winter Sun*, p. 8)

New Life

Meiotic cell division special for,
  Producing gametes needed for new life.
Like an immortal casting of the dice,
  To bring ancestral traits up to the fore.

These sexual gametes from our moms and dads,
  Are stored until released through intercourse.
From dad, two hundred million streaming for,
  The solitary package mom provides.

Then starts what some might call a true romance.
  Imagine all these millions in a race,
The goal, one oocyte that mom provides,
  They shift, and turn, propelled by churning ends.

When single sperm cell meets the oocyte,
  The curtain falls, the rest are left to die.
Then starts romance within the oocyte,
  Things never will be quite the same again.

The elements within the sperm and egg,
  Mingle in a lifelong dual dance.
Henceforth, all the structures that ensue,
  Will replicate the mix of this embrace.

Amniotic fluid, that warm bath,
  Protects, as growth takes over, the next stage,
Tissue, organs, systems generate,
  Form and motion next predominate.

Maternal circulation freely flows,
  Through umbilicus to sustain the life,
That is developing in mother's womb,
  Until the signal that its time to move.

The pangs of birth are known so well to mom,
  Then quick forgotten when new life appears.
Mother, baby, father, love so dear,
  Like Father, Son, and Holy Spirit share.

(from *Casting About*, p. 76)

Sunlight

Our sun, that glorious star, God's hand has shown.
  Created when the universe gave birth.
The source of life, this wondrous light has thrown.

No life can be, unless our sun has shone,
  And life from shining sun has shown its worth.
Our sun, that glorious star, God's hand has shown.

Plants will grow wherever seeds are sown,
  As sun shines down around our world's girth,
The source of life, this wondrous light has thrown.

And animals, where prior plants have grown,
  And fish within the waters of the firth,
Our sun, that glorious star, God's hand has shown.

And then came man, atop creations throne.
  Our sun provides the warmth, God's lavish hearth,
The source of life, this wondrous light has thrown.

We humans should be thankful God has known,
  Our needs for joy and gladness, and of mirth,
Our sun, that glorious star, God's hand has shown.
  The source of life, this wondrous light has thrown.

(from *The Open Door,* p. 89)

42

Awesome

Awesome is a word I often hear,
  Used by kids or grandkids to describe,
A happening, oft trite, that they undear,
  Or vibes of music to which they subscribe.

But toss the reach of mind and heart out far.
  Be venturesome, and curious, as you tread.
And know there is a height to set the bar.
  Attainment helps to keep a step ahead.

There's puzzle and uncertainty out there.
  Unfathomed mystery ever to survey.
Wonderment and beauty everywhere.
  Evoking new excitement every day.

Our universe is awesome, be aware,
God's creation meant for us to share.

(from *Winter Sun*, p. 33)

Fog

Ten miles out from Washington's northern coast,
  Pacific waters calm, a sunny day.
The salmon fishing good, we caught a few,
  Then fog came in, so dense, the bow unseen.

We had to wend our way to Neah Bay,
  Through rock outcrop, and danger-ridden shoals.
We slowly picked our way, and prayed a lot,
  With compass, chart, and sounder for the depth.

The ship of life to reach far distant shore,
  Can learn a lesson from a ship at sea.
Know where we are, and where we want to be,
  And be alert to pray along the way.

The fog of life is still another thing.
  Beware, it may be there, but still unseen.
Be cautious if this fog is settling,
  We need to reach safe harbor in one piece.

(from *Casting About* ,p. 86)

Diversity

Throughout our world we see life as diverse.
  Plants provide a cornucopia.
Various grains and fruits does nature nurse,
  For nutrient needs, creation's bold idea.

Animals too, we see in wide array,
  Cattle, hogs and hens, meat, eggs and milk.
Oxen pull, and horse to ride and dray,
  And wild beasts and birds of varied ilk.

Why should it be surprising to see man,
  Atop creation's ladder, yet diverse.
God's way of showing off His superb plan.
  Let differences astound, not be averse.

Diversity in man, a glorious trait.
Inscrutable, God's will to so create.

(from *The Open Door,* p. 90)

Time

Ethereal quantum, known when we are born.
  Days and years mark where we were before.
Circuit and rotation standard for,
  That time is earth dependent, furthermore.

If perched on other planets time is skewed.
  The marian year, six hundred earthly days,
While Venus rotates once two hundred days.
  Sleep and birthdays problems to keep tuned.

Does time exist outside of planet's moves?
  Would speed of light be standard bearer then?
But distance per earth's second, light depends,
  Its timing, earth dependent once again.

But our Creator could have other thought.
  That earthly motion be dependent on,
The metabolic needs of life to come,
  And time on earth subserve the needs of man.

(from *Casting About*, p. 75)

Winter Flowers

February, dreary month at best.
  Midwinter slog, some snow much rain to drench.
Grey skies dark days at this our winter's crest.
  Cold winds blow, our spirits they do wrench.

And then one day we see the buds expand,
  Camellia bushes around the house all start,
Red, then pink, now white, unfurling grand,
  These hardy buds, snow caps they push apart.

A few more days these bushes color wreathed,
  The earliest winter flowers at our stead.
Our spirits welcome flowers, now unsheathed,
  Earliest sign of spring await ahead.

Crocus, tulip, daffodil are weeks away,
But camellias separate us from winter's grey.

(from *Winter Sun*, p. 4)

The Search

The Search

We humans who inhabit planet earth,
  We have this yen to question, and to search.
We poke around until we can unearth,
  Our whereabouts, what gave us this our perch.

Creator God has helped us on the way.
  He has revealed Himself to searching man.
Prophets, covenants, we should obey,
  Until unfolds for us God's saving plan.

Three persons as one God, was then revealed.
  Father, Word, and Spirit, then made known.
Man's future rests with God, this God has sealed.
  The Word, made Jesus, He is our keystone.

Our search is now completed, God of powers.
We are eternal, and You God now are ours.

Self

Are we but outlines, images of ourselves,
  For others to survey as they see fit?
We cater to what others from their shelves
  Can add to our enhancement, bit by bit.

Sometimes we make our image what it isn't,
  More than what it is by some degree,
Confounding what we are and what we shouldn't,
  Becoming thus, a mere menagerie.

Our inner self becomes confused by this,
  Shrunken twisted spirit meant to be,
Happy, but no longer, where is bliss?
  Can we no longer shape our destiny?

Affirm the inner self as sovereign space,
Don't let others' thoughts purloin our place.

(from *Casting About*, p. 16)

Justice

Justice stirs within the soul and mind,
  An attitude for ever rendering,
Righteousness toward others, never blind,
  To trust and equity, surrendering.

Justice treats the just self as another,
  Fair minded as how things are meted out.
Others as a sister or a brother,
  And total love for God without a doubt.

Render unto God, but what to render?
  All love, all hope, all trust, in faith to tender;
Then what is left? Who does become the vendor?
  And with such transfer who becomes the spender?

All mankind benefits in just transaction,
Mercy and Justice kiss, God's benefaction.

Useless

It is a mind set leaving one adrift.
  A feel of hopelessness, of chronic dread.
Of whether one can butter one's own bread.
  Unsure of when to stay or when to shift.
The world manipulates and seeks to lift
  In varied fields of play, thrills to be bred.
Useless ones left in the cold to tread,
  No gift to spend on trash. Be gone, be swift.

Cold and heartless world, bereft of aid.
  Yet hope belongs a world apart, above.
God, creator, rends this cruel fate,
  Solace, succor to those who might have strayed.
As Milton* says about abiding love,
  "They also serve who only stand and wait."

*John Milton (1608-1674)
Sonnet: "On His Blindness"

(from *The Open Door.* p. 106)

Mistakes

We all make them,
  These blunders on our way.
Learning for the future,
  Preparing for the fray.

They are a part of learning,
  Identify as such.
The man who's never erred,
  Has never learned that much.

Be honest, and admit,
  Those mistakes we've made.
Others then can help,
  We shouldn't be afraid.

To nullify our errors,
  Or deny they're ours,
Sullies our existence,
  Falsifies our hours.

Be brave with our mistakes.
  If we don't reach first base,
Know if we keep trying,
  We'll find our rightful place.

(from *Winter Sun*, p. 25)

Fear of the Lord

I really don't know what to make of this.
To love entirely our Father God.
And our savior Jesus I applaud,
I know that heaven is a place of bliss.
I also know that there is an abyss,
A hell place meant for those who are outlawed,
But heaven is our home, and I am awed,
I hope in this, but might I run amiss?

Perhaps I have not thought this through enough.
Am I remiss in thinking it's my call?
I cannot save myself, I do need aid,
The Holy Spirit holds me by the scruff,
My fear should be that He would let me fall,
With love and fear I will not be afraid.

Idols

They're all around, these things we idolize,
  My suit, my car, my cell, my diamond brooch,
Or tickets to the ball game we so prize,
  Or things our lives encounter, then encroach.

We sometimes wish too much for whim so near,
  Then envy others having what we lack.
We steal, or lust, or crave for what is dear,
  Let greed or angry pride take us aback.

Its not the things themselves that lead astray,
  Our lust to self possess gets in the way.
We have to sell our soul, then become prey,
  A dreadful turn, our freedom gone away.

In idolizing things we let them take,
Our inmost self, our soul, theirs to remake.

(from *The Open Door*, p. 84)

Darkness

Pitch blackness, we're inside without a light.
  Disorienting, unfamiliar space.
Moving, any direction, brings on fright,
  Nothing to touch, uncertain of our place.

What to do to find our way outside?
  Crawling on the floor might help us yet,
To find a wall or door to be our guide,
  And help us to avoid an unseen threat.

Where soul and mind are cloaked in dark affairs,
  And sadness supplants joy at every turn,
An inner light we need to sidestep errors,
  And find a bright new pathway, ours to churn.

If darkness leaves our soul in such distress,
Pray for inner light to give egress.

(from *The Open Door.* p. 93)

Sin

Sin through human eyes is but a blur,
  Its borders indistinct, its depth unsure,
Plato writes of virtue: do no harm,
  While evil has its clutches on the earth.

Evil abounds in this wide world of ours,
  Famine flood and fire take their toll.
But sin is something else, our conscience knows
  Put there by God, a law within our souls.

We cannot grasp the horror that is sin,
  Unless we vision it through God's own eyes.
Sinful man, immortal though he be,
  Is banned from God for all eternity.

With sin, man turns his will away from God,
  Unwanted, God is but a hindrance.
Shackles placed on mankind: avarice,
  Pride, envy, gluttony, sloth, anger, lust.

To rescue man required a terrible price,
  The death of God's own Son in sacrifice.
Took blood of Jesus to remove sin's stain,
  Since man unable to make up the gain.

Jesus did far more than sacrifice,
  He brought us grace to combat future sin.
The light, the life, the truth, the way, He gave,
  To defeat death, and gain eternal bliss.

The channels of this grace, the sacraments,
  Himself supreme in Holy Eucharist.
Prayer provides relationship, divine,
  The armor for the battle we all fight.

Hate sin, as God hates sin. A Savior's blood,
  Was shed to compensate the awful warp,
Produced by sin within the soul of man.
  Stay vigilant! God's grace wins in the end.

(from *Casting About*, p. 44)

Purgatory

That old shirt, too good to throw away.
  Your father's father, and your father too,
Wore it, long before your time was due.
  It's made of wondrous fabric, don't you see.

I know that all my angel says is true,
  With buttons off the front and off the cuff.
The shoulder's torn, and there are spots galore,
  From where I changed the oil on the car.

I know a place just miles down the street.
  Angel Cleaners, they will take and treat,
To clean and mend, and make your shirt like new.
  So come with me, and I will take you through.

The door was open, and I walked right in.
  My name is Gabriel, can I be of use?
This shirt within my family many years,
  I bring to see if it can be renewed.

It may be too far gone, but could you try,
  To mend the shoulder, and remove the spots,
And find new buttons for the cuff and front,
  To replace those that have long since been lost.

Michael, he the strong, will work the tear,
  The fibers will be woven, not just sewn.
Uriel will remove the spots with soaks,
  His eye sees everything that could remain.

Raphael will match buttons, as before,
  His healing touch will sew them all in place.
When we are through your shirt should be like new,
  But let me warn you of the things we do.

Be prepared that it will take much time,
  To do the things that here I have outlined.
If unable to achieve these tasks,
  Your shirt will burn with all the other trash.

(from *Casting About,* p. 46)

Promise

There are those pledges made into thin air,
  From futile yearnings failure has laid bare,
Thwarted doings, shame has brought its share
  Aimless ruse forsaken ones do bear.

Bottom of the heap, a fall so far.
  Others too have fallen, though not near.
Alone, we feel our life on rocks, ajar,
  Is this the end of life, abyss to fear?

But pledge can be the start of something new,
  A promise that with strength, we'll see this through.
But strength from where? A needed type of glue.
  A place to stand, a different kind of queue.

Pledge can be a prayer for needed force,
A strength to guide us on a new sought course.

(from *Winter Sun*, p. 22)

Suffering

It is the lot of humankind to feel,
  The burden that is suffering, as we strive.
Pain and anguish oft do make us reel,
  Replacing joy and peace till we revive.

We do not want to think of these our blues,
  And oft we seek relief from any source,
If drugs or alcohol are what we choose,
  A private hell may be our future course.

Why God? We often ask, while suffering.
  In asking, we may want instant relief.
Anger toward our God, admonishing,
  May thus seep in, and add unending grief.

We do not know why suffering is rife.
But should not blame our God in this our life.

(from *The Open Door*, p. 96)

Conscience

We each have deep inside a compass true
  To help us tell the difference, right from wrong.
Our conscience, placed by God, in play lifelong,
  Unerring if it's properly used anew.
It points out wrong, then leads us to eschew,
  Evil as the place we don't belong.
But if we choose an evil way, headstrong,
  Then good is left asunder, all askew.

If we tell our conscience to stand clear,
  And rush to do things all alone, our way,
Confusion will result, an inner fog.
  We run afoul of all that we've held dear,
And from our former path we're led astray,
  A wayward never-ending wanton slog.

Knowledge

The urge to know forthwith, a person trait.
  For plants and animals a hopeless quest.
Knowledge piled on knowledge, persons stressed,
  While overload becomes a thing to hate.
Automation brings a kind of sate,
  Tools ever using without rest,
A potpourri from which we feel pressed,
  And knowledge then a burden, useless freight.

We human persons have a need to know.
  But if we open wide the intake door,
We're tossed as flotsam on this ocean's wave,
  At risk of being lost on random shoal.
Rest and ponder, sort what's good, and store,
  Throw overboard the rest as trash to waive.

The Open Door

The open door will beckon us inside.
  But only if we venture to be free,
To step across the barrier of our pride.

One foot at a time should be our stride.
  Confront temptation that would have us flee.
The open door will beckon us inside.

And don't look back from this which we have tried.
  Our happiness, and destiny will be,
To step across the barrier of our pride.

If we should choose, instead, to stay outside,
  But find that pain and sorrow the decree,
The open door will beckon us inside.

If we try to plant each foot astride,
  The threshold, we may then be blind to see,
To step across the barrier of our pride.

Let not worldly things for us decide,
  That which humbly we could all foresee.
The open door will beckon us inside.
  To step across the barrier of our pride.

(from *The Open Door,* p. 73)

Understanding

Knowing is in seeing the connections,
  Of ways that persons think of many things.
We use our minds to search for new directions,
  Perceived as good in what our thinking brings.

This is a process mind and soul engage.
  Not just a piling up that data lends.
We piece together, refining, then assuage,
  What this new linkage means, how it portends.

Our minds are restless, onward they must go.
  The search is ever on for perceived gain.
But gain for self, or others, that's a throe,
  The gain for good or evil, to attain.

Use our thinking minds to understand,
And posit good. Let evil then be banned.

Redemption

To be redeemed, the need is a redeemer,
  A person, not a thing who's free to act.
As human persons we need a contract,
  As this cannot be only our affair.
It needs a person for our faults to bear.
  From all humanity, sins to extract.
And who in justice pays the price exact.
  Thus, God alone, a daunting feat to share.

The price was terrible, a painful death,
  Then to His heart was thrust a soldier's lance.
And three days later rose again Our Lord.
  We need to know Our Lord gave His last breath,
And need be always thankful for this chance,
  For He has given all He could afford.

(And thus a blessing, a beatitude)

Religion

Religion is about relationships,
  A systematic body of connections.
Religion, thus a science, comes to grips,
  And like all science, searches for directions.

The conflict between science and religion,
  Like sibling rivalry, because of closeness,
Both search for truth, with strict articulation,
  Foregoing falsity, and all absurdness.

Science and religion have been scammed.
  Charlatans and frauds, who ply their schemes,
For notoriety or profit, truth be damned,
  Leaving masses shorn of truth and dreams.

Religion and all science should align,
To search out truth and goodness to enshrine.

(from *The Open Door*, p. 83)

There Are No Atheists

Do not think I'm looney when I say,
  There are no atheists. Of course there are.
The notion comes from way back and afar,
  With soldiers facing doom, a hopeless fray.
Nineteen forty two, and theirs' to weigh,
  On Bataan's broad expanse their plight bizarre.
They pondered fate, awaiting the crowbar,
  From deep in foxholes where those soldiers lay.

Out of food and bullets, Starved and shorn,
  Of arms that might have kept them in the fight.
The future grim, they faced a cruel foe.
  "No atheists in the foxholes" then was born,
The quote which one therein was quick to write.
  Impending doom leaves God a welcome glow.

The Trinity

What do we know of this our Triune God?
  Not everything, but still we know a lot.
Eternal, three in persons, one so awed.

Creator of the universe we laud,
  From nothing to the present He has brought.
What do we know of this our triune God?

All about our God we should applaud,
  Creation of humanity He bought.
Eternal, three in persons, one so awed.

But human persons turned, we were thus flawed.
  But God did not abandon, rather sought.
What do we know of this our triune God?

To the rescue, we who were outlawed,
  Salvation of humanity He wrought.
Eternal, three in persons, one so awed.

He wants humanity to give its nod,
  And live our lives as He wants, this our ought.
What do we know of this our triune God?
  Eternal, three in persons, one so awed.

The Good Life

The Good LIfe

The good life ushers in a peaceful end.
  A life well lived should ever satisfy.
Seek always paths that do not thus offend.

Honor, truth, and goodness, worthy blend;
  These for you, they do not lead awry.
The good life ushers in a peaceful end.

Patience, kindness, gentleness, depend
  On mind and will enlivened to comply
Seek always paths that do not thus offend.

Be modest, self control'd do not pretend,
  Then joy and peace will enter and apply,
The good life ushers in a peaceful end.

Be chaste and faithful, wonders God will send,
  Be steadfast, clean of heart, these certify,
Seek always paths that do not thus offend.

Let virtues stay with you, yours to befriend,
  Endure, keep them within, they gratify,
The good life ushers in a peaceful end.
  Seek always paths that do not thus offend.

Prudence

We have a lodestar deep within our core,
  Hidden, not of body, but of soul.
Conscience, placed by God, a bell to toll,
  If danger lurks, a balance to restore.
This is a guide, a never ending chore,
  To keep us free from harm, our person whole.
To keep from floundering on evil's shoal,
  We need to stay alert, and ply the oar.

From thence comes Prudence, lodestar's ponderer,
  Is there to search and sift assorted wares.
Best from worst, or right from wrong to forge,
  To point the way, and not allow disorder.
Use often, best accompanied with prayers.
  Keep valued goods, all refuse then disgorge.

The Unbending Road

Keep footfalls press'd on this unbending road.
  Always onward, don't be led astray,
Then heaven's glory waits, a new abode.

You then, home free, will be, with nothing owed,
  And not be left outside with feet of clay.
  Keep footfalls press'd on this unbending road.

All humanity have ever flowed,
  Upon this throughway, paved to walk and pray,
Then heaven's glory waits, a new abode.

Virtue guards from slippage, evil's goad,
  To waylay off the path, then turn away,
Keep footfalls press'd on this unbending road.

Prudence, justice, fortitude, all toed,
  With temperance, sure guides, for all to weigh,
Then heaven's glory waits, a new abode.

Don't let virtue's guard rails thus erode,
  Lest toward perdition evil leads the way,
Keep footfalls press'd on this unbending road,
  Then heaven's glory waits, a new abode.

Fortitude

The Roman arch has strength beyond belief,
  Support of walls and doors in ancient time.
The human foot an arch for one's lifetime,
  Our body's weight it bears, the same motif.
Fortitude bespeaks of strength as well,
  But is not thereby bound by strength alone.
A brace against temptation its capstone,
  Constancy for good within, does dwell.

Obstacles are overcome by it,
  Fear is lessened or abolished though,
Persecution tolerated, yet,
  Fortitude will last, and never quit.
Firm when difficulties bring on woe,
  Strength against adversity and threat.

Strength

Strength is standing as a brace against,
  Whatever might displace the holding place.
Stalwart pillar providing a defense,
  Repelling chaos aiming to deface.

Strength is gentleness, no need to brag,
  Vigor for right paths leads not astray,
Sustenance for when we tend to lag,
  And fortitude, our weakness to defray.

Strength, a patient stance against the storm.
  Stand, await the coming of the calm,
Though the conflict difficult and warm,
  The storm will pass, await the healing balm.

Strength is not vainglory on display,
A virtue, humble, steadfast, its array.

(from *Winter Sun*, p. 19)

Temperance

Live well, but keep the appetites in check,
  For appetites amok can lead to ruin.
This situation leaves the soul a wreck
  Confused, uncertain, failing from within.

Temperance has mastery over things.
  Pleasure has its grace when kept in place.
Moderation thus a balance brings,
  The soul thus free, the excess to efface.

Temperance gives mastery when in doubt,
  Base instincts not allow'd to supersede.
Evil then is left, a wailful shout,
  While honor, truth and goodness thereby freed.

Keep footfalls press'd on this unbending road,
Let temperance be guide, the mother lode.

Faith

Faith demands a system of belief.
  Belief of what? Its origin from whence?
From God alone, His only to dispense,
  Pure gift, cannot be bought, and thus our lief.
Love God and others as ourselves in brief,
  Contains the basics, is so simple, hence,
Believe or not believe, a choice so tense,
  Abandoning the gift may lead to grief.

Believers seek to know and do God's will,
  Committing self entirely to God,
And trusting that the faith is based on truth.
  Faith is living, guiding lives, until,
Departure comes, we praise and give our laud,
  Then find, for certain, faith has been our sooth.

Hope

Hopeless is the man condemned to death,
  As he awaits the noose around his neck.
Soon there will be only one last breath.
  His pleas exhausted, then the call and beck.

Hope is placed by God in all of us,
  A yen for happiness beyond this life.
A yearning without proof, but known, and thus,
  To suffer for what's good, and bear all strife.

Precious hope is solid if we stay,
  Within the bounds of goodness consciously.
But if we falter and leave hope at bay,
  We may then wander, puzzled, hopelessly.

Best to take this gift of hope and hold,
It deep within, more precious than pure gold.

Charity

Charity, an overarching reach,
  Encompassing all virtue in its grip.
Its buoyancy, an ever upward trip,
  But absence leaves a void, a lifelong breach.
What then has charity for us to teach?
  It is the gift of love from God's kingship
Central to our souls, He does equip
  As guide and proven avenue for each.

Love God above all else, and others too,
  As thyself; a new law passed, to heed.
Obey our God in love, this is our quest,
  Believe and hope, be gentle, and be true,
Rejoice in right, bear all things, this we need,
  The course is love, depend on this, be blessed.

Truth

Truth, the power of enlightenment.
  The antonym of shams, half-truths, and lies.
Eternal, it proclaims God's covenant.

Search, and ye shall find in scripture meant,
  Ponder patiently to find the prize.
Truth, the power of enlightenment.

A lifetime may be spent in this ascent,
  And sometimes there is need to compromise,
Eternal, it proclaims God's covenant.

Beware a masquerade where truth is bent,
  False pretending, posturing, a guise,
Truth, the power of enlightenment.

When found, internalize, 'tis heaven sent,
  Truth, the hallmark of the truly wise.
Eternal, it proclaims God's covenant.

It vanquishes all falseness in dissent,
  Honor, hope, and goodness, its allies
Truth, the power of enlightenment.
  Eternal, it proclaims God's covenant.

Wisdom

Wisdom comes from heaven, and is pure,
  It breathes of mercy, peace, sincerity,
Contentment, happiness, its raiment sure,
  All contained in close proximity.

Wisdom is not blind, does not seek wealth,
  Is not self-seeking, knows from whence it came,
Disdains deceit, does not partake in stealth,
  Tranquility and goodness its acclaim.

Those without can only ask and pray,
  For wisdom is a gift from heaven's loft.
It comes so gradually, 'tis heaven's way,
  Accumulates with age, a gentle waft.

Treasure wisdom, never let it go,
Planted, nourished, slowly it will grow.

Happiness

Whenever in this life we do find joy,
  Brief though this encounter seems to be,
Seek the wellspring, first, and then enjoy,
  And know that God, the source, can lead us free.

Sadness, the antithesis of bliss,
  Accompanies vexation ever near,
Depression then, may lead to an abyss,
  Seek the wellspring, from depression veer.

Humankind is meant for happiness,
  While suffering is felt along the way,
Given by our God, our life to bless,
  Suffering with joy, a mix to stay.

Commit ourselves to God, to Him endear,
Engulfed in Mercy, there's no more to fear.

Joy

Joy does not fray nerves with forlorn high,
  Nor plummet onto jagged rocks below.
Things when hooked on, furtively to buy,
  While lingering use brings misery and woe.

Joy's presence brings a warming inner glow.
  A feel of love and goodness, no dismay,
Lasting contentment, a power does bestow,
  While fear and frantic feelings kept at bay.

Joy, a heavenly presence meant to be,
  Buoyancy along life's winding path.
Beneficence to last, felicity,
  Does not give way to sadness, or to wrath.

Pray this wondrous gift of joy will stay,
To guide us on life's journey, not astray.

(from *The Open Door*, p. 82)

Peace

Peace encountered deep within the soul.
  Tranquility, companion on the way,
A path from which we do not want to stray,
  But stay, and leave us thereby in control.
Yet outer factors change, and take their toll,
  Some are scalding hot, our souls to flay,
Disorder and discord then theirs to stay,
  An inner hell has forced us from our goal.

Lashing out against unreal foe,
  Is commonplace, though enemy within.
Encounter leads to strife, enabling,
  Forging groups for battle, looming woe.
Peace the victim, should such strife begin,
  And desolation would such action bring.

Patience

Patience teaches souls how to endure,
  To bear with tolerance all adverse woe.
To not be swayed, or waylaid, by allure,
  Forbear, when troubles brew, keep soul aglow.

The stoics weigh and bear adversity,
  Without external change in their demean.
They take what comes with equanimity,
  And show no sign that such would cause a scene.

Most of us when dealt with suffering,
  Might wince or cringe, the imprint on our face.
So human, to react while struggling,
  Yet patience to endure, a heavenly grace.

Meet adversity and bravely know,
Restraint, remaining calm, is ours to show.

Ode to Kindness

Erato, muse of poets, help me out.
  Awake in ancient Greece from your long sleep.
I need a poem, a theme to write about,
  Ideas that if given I might keep.
Little one you have aroused my heart.
  What would you have me do for you today?
    I want to write of kindness, yet
      Don't know how to start.
Lend your wisdom that I may not stray
  Your gift would be forever in my debt.

Kindness, little one, a noble theme,
  Let's start with the ingredients forthwith,
Ingredients, Erato? Do I dream?
  Patience, little one, be a wordsmith.
Let's use the metaphor of baking bread,
  Flour, water, salt and leavening,
    Kindness is of love and goodness
      Stir and incubate ahead.
Keep deep inside your soul, no editing,
  Like expanding bread in space a fullness.

Erato, muse of poets, thank you much,
  So simple, kindness is a gracious mix
Of love and goodness, others with it touch.
  Kindness then to others will affix.
Know, little one, that I am but a myth.
  If a person, bodied with a soul,
    I would, like you, obey and worship
      Our God of all, forthwith.
I have inspired Homer and his scroll,
  So now I must return, no further script.

Be Good

Good bye, ta ta, adios, adieu, au revoir
  Though language differs, they all mean the same,
Salutations said when going far,
  Stay good until we meet again, our aim.

Beauty in the words and sentiment,
  Mutual prayer expressed, though brief in words.
Love and goodness twined in fond moment,
  Hearts of one accord, goodness conferred.

But can we stretch this heartfelt goodness far,
  And search for burning embers of good there,
Where others, even strangers, smoldering are,
  And offer up to all a heartfelt prayer?

Towers of babble leave confusions ware,
While goodness trumps contention, ours to share.

(from *Winter Sun*, p. 34)

Self Control

Lessons gained in learning how to drive,
  May save you when you get behind the wheel.
Learn to brake and steer, for these do strive,
  And limit speed, stay safe, these have appeal.

Those lessons learned, a way to self control,
  Will help assure a happy, peaceful life.
Learn to steer around each bumpy shoal,
  And slow or stop to lessen future strife.

Habits learned while driving one's own car,
  Require repetition to excel.
Know self control in life is our lodestar,
  So dedicate to this and ever dwell.

Mastery of self a foremost quest,
A life so lived has zest and will be blessed.

Gentleness

Before Erato left I asked again,
  Can you bespeak once more, of gentleness?
Little one, you want verbosity?
  No time, let us keep conversation plain.
Gentleness inhabits those who reign,
  Of self alone, no grandiosity,
They have no need for false pomposity
  Gentle giants are without disdain.

Gentle ones possess an inner peace
  Strength they have, no further need or fuss
Quiet happy lives they do express
  With that Erato left for ancient Greece
I'm glad he stayed around to help discuss
  How gentleness is what we can possess.

Chastity

Is sexuality Creator blessed?
  Of course! It is creative in its act.
Then why if it is central in our quest,
  Do many run afoul of this same fact?

Control of self behavior is the key.
  If pleasure is the only norm in play,
It starts a slide to vast uncertainty,
  And damage is to persons, evil's way.

Purity of mind and soul ring true,
  A pledge of faithful living ever so,
Then difficulties, rampant, ever new,
  Will not distort the course, a grace to know.

Two are needed for creation's path,
Faithful each to each will forestall wrath.

Ode to Modesty

Why be modest when our culture cries
  For self fulfillment earned at any cost.
Pursue whatever works to gain the prize
  No matter should our goodness then be lost.
Attain and overcome, a constant goal,
  Let others in the way be pushed aside,
    To their demise,
      In our control.
The world is ours, a tribute to our pride,
  To take whatever moves before our eyes.

And yet such brash behavior causes harm.
  Others suffer at our whim and call.
Our inner soul may signal, and alarm,
  Such wanton gain may lead to our downfall.
What gain is this if in the end we lose
  All self respect, and our immortal soul?
    Desist from evil ways,
      And don't abuse.
God's grace is ours, and then we will be whole,
  And stay within the purview of God's gaze.

Be modest, though the culture does cry out.
  An unassuming mien lets you be free.
The humble person, peaceful, does not shout,
  And bears an inner calm, tranquility.
Be true to self, ask what your conscience knows,
  And follow what is good and honorable,
    Avoid indecency,
      Yourself compose.
Then inner strength will be unconquerable,
  Your life will have a new proficiency.

Generosity

Does giving equal generosity?
  Or are there deeper values that portend.
And what of the amount that givers spend.
  Do givers expect reciprocity?
Some may give in plain pomposity,
  And wave the check just written they have penned,
But give so very little in the end,
  While acting with misused jocosity.

Generous is giving with a touch,
  It may be from the pocket or the heart.
If only from the pocket, may be scant,
  Spare change only, therefore not that much.
But giving till it hurts, a thing apart,
  One's wants for others' needs, it does supplant.

Blood and Water

The lance that drew the blood from Jesus' side,
  Spewed water from His Heart with blood as well.
A fount of mercy poured when Jesus died.

Was this a pouring out of grace beside?
  A faithful shower shown to ever tell?
The lance that drew the blood from Jesus' side.

Father forgive, His mercy was applied,
  As hanging on the cross He said farewell,
A fount of mercy poured when Jesus died.

But what to us this slaughter should provide?
  To put our faith in this, and ever dwell.
The lance that drew the blood from Jesus' side.

The water used to wash our sins aside,
  His blood for our salvation did compel,
A fount of mercy poured when Jesus died.

Let blood and water ever be our guide,
  To place our trust in this, and thus compel.
The lance that drew the blood from Jesus' side,
  A fount of mercy poured when Jesus died.

Freedom

Ah, that wondrous word that lets us be,
  Free to choose, that is our given right.
But if we choose a wild buying spree,
  We learn we cannot have all in our sight.

Does freedom "from" allow us to live free?
  Free from pain and death, no guarantee,
From poverty and sickness, wait and see,
  From toil and sorrow, this is not to be.

The freedom seen above is freedom chained.
  What is left? What is it to be free?
Immortality, when lost or gained,
  A soul thing, extending through eternity.

Difficult to grasp, but we can sing:
Keep freedom true to its immortal ring.

(from *The Open Door*, p. 123)

Grace

A power beyond our sight or other sense.
  I'll liken it to sunlight, which we see.
No life on earth unless our sun dispense,
  Its rays for plant and animal as key.

Grace envelopes earth in much that way.
  Selective for the human heart and soul.
Unlike the sun it reaches night and day.
  Its power, like the sun, to keep us whole.

We can escape the sun by seeking shade,
  But grace finds us, unless we run apart,
But if we turn and rue that we have strayed,
  Grace will find us for another start.

Grace we need to keep our souls alive.
Abandon grace and we cannot survive.

Personhood

What does it mean to be a human person?
  Do other living things share this domain?
And what about being bodied does this worsen?
  If not persons, what have they to gain?

Our bodies, like all other living things,
  Wither and decay, become debris.
From plants and animals this backdrop springs,
  All nature knows of death, no bodies free.

Three Persons in one God the Trinity.
  Three in one, eternal, is the core.
Man created for infinity.
  Human, bodied souls, forevermore.

Our souls to God more precious than our flesh.
Yet bodies to be resurrected fresh.

War

As this is written look around and see.
  Do any on this planet know not war?
It inundates us all, its ugly gore,
  A cloud around from which we cannot flee.
Then at war's end we utter wanton plea
  Might this be all? A closing of this door?
But Cerberus, the dog of war, wants more.
  Death awaits, the wailing, the banshee.

What must we see before all wars could end?
  To know the seeds of war are from within.
Power, greed, and lust we should abhor,
  To root these from our souls we need attend.
Then peace and lasting solace, might begin,
  A blessing, beatitude, forevermore.

Ode to Holiness

Holiness, a trip in space unseen.
  Eyes and ears provide no help with this,
And touch cannot provide a clue, a screen,
  To thus envision what might be amiss.
We risk our future here and then beyond,
  If we do not partake of holiness.
    To learn of what it means,
      And why we should respond.
A start, humility, our lowliness,
  Will help establish where this viewpoint leans.

There is no holiness without a God,
  And none, unless there is the Trinity.
To this we must be genuinely awed,
  Three Persons bound in one Divinity.
Then realize beyond our earth's domain,
  There is a heaven, and alas a hell,
    To dwell in one eternal,
      And thus attain.
Holiness portends heaven we shall dwell,
  And be removed from hell, that site infernal.

But what is holiness from sight unseen?
  It is a grace from God that sanctifies.
Our souls are swept by God and rendered clean,
  No sin remains, thus precious in God's eyes.
Baptism takes sin from out our soul,
  Then penance when and if we sin again,
    Our souls remain sin free,
      Our heavenly goal.
As God is holy, we should say amen,
  And thank our God the Holy Trinity.

Holiness

What is that which goodness does beget?
  A state akin, and has it in its debt.
Goodness lived can shed the remnants of,
  Evil all around, but from above,
Comes grace, that freely flows where goodness is,
  Forcing evil back to its abyss.

Words can be applied in varied ways.
  When formed in prayer, they flow in upward praise.
Thankful to be free, to move in strength.
  Stretching out in breadth and width and length.
Unrestricted joyful peaceful states.
  Holiness, the mantle that awaits.

Evil has its ploy against all this,
  Barriers that make holiness remiss,
"Holier than thou" it calls across,
  Or "goody goody", to the young a toss,
When youth is growing, to its own does cling,
  While evil does inflict its cruel sting.

Be brave, be stalwart, ever vigilant,
  Be prayerful daily, ever diligent.
Love goodness for itself, love does not fail,
  To strengthen in the way of all travail.
Then holiness will with its mantle bring,
  True freedom and protection, heaven's ring.

Be not afraid to live in holiness.
  Authentic path to stable happiness.

(from *Winter Sun*, p. 68)

Faithfulness

What does faith mean in times so turbulent?
  To place our faith in something beyond self.
It means we trust, a lasting testament.
  Belief in something for and of itself.

It speaks of love and truth and sacrifice.
  A willingness to suffer hurt and pain.
To risk beyond the now, at any price.
  And put aside what would be one's own gain.

Honor, family, country, these we pledge,
  Our willingness to stand, not run afar,
And to our God in keeping we allege,
  We will be true to conscience, God's lodestar.

"Semper Fidelis", young marines are taught,
"Always faithful", doing what they ought.

Pray

In prayer we raise our hearts to Christ our Lord.
  And to the Father, Spirit, the Godhead.
Our prayer then twined for all the world's accord,

Salvation is God's work, He brings us toward,
  His passion, death, and rising, table spread,
In prayer we raise our hearts to Christ our Lord.

With contrite humble hearts our Lord adored,
  With Christ's own bread, the Eucharist, we are fed,
Our prayers then twined for all the world's accord.

Adoring, praising, loving, we afford,
  Our prayer, thus simple, words need not be said,
In prayer we raise our hearts to Christ our Lord.

And we should ask God's help when we're ignored,
  When troubles brew, or we are seeped in dread,
Our prayer then twined for all the world's accord.

We have this need, an inner resonant chord,
  From deep within our marrow, a search ahead.
In prayer we raise our hearts to Christ our Lord.
  Our prayer then twined for all the world's accord.

Prayer

We have this yearning to communicate,
  The fibers of our selves participate,
Texting has become obsession bent,
  Nanoseconds in exchanges spent.

While listening to Legende by Caplet,
  A young girl sat the row in front with thumbs,
A-twittering on her cell phone busily,
  Multi-tasking communicatively.

Prayer, a form of nexus, linking us,
  To God, and forebears who are heavenly,
Needs scrutiny to see what this should be,
  Why should we pray? Why waste such energy?

Remember, all on earth belong to God.
  He wants for us to come to Him in prayer,
For needed help to reach our destiny,
  To be with Him for all eternity.

Prayer has many forms, let's look at these.
  Can be as brief as Jesus, said alone,
Or short refrains, as Jesus I trust Thee.
  They can be said all day repeatedly.

Some should be memorized for ease of use.
  The Creed, our Father, and the Glory Be.
The Hail Mary, these four, make it be.
  Say them morning, night, throughout the day.

The rosary, gift to Saint Dominic,
  That glorious string of ave's, grouped in tens,
Portrays the life of Jesus, birth to end,
  Worth your while to pray it when you can.

The Catholic mass and Holy Eucharist,
  God's gift of Self, to help along the way.
We please and honor God with this array,
  Divine relationship, come let us pray.

(from *Casting about*, p. 50)

Ascension

And what did Our Lord do when He arose?
  He showed Himself and stayed for forty days.
He could have done whatever He then chose,
  Instead He slowly rose to crowded gaze.

He left with sacraments and words in place,
  To a small band of followers enshrined,
His vehicle on earth, a special grace,
  His living church a sign for all mankind.

Salvation thus extended to the world.
  The church to blossom, and extend His reach,
And keep from clutches of the netherworld.
  Believe and follow, everywhere to preach.

Thus a blessing, and beatitude.
God's lasting covenant again renewed.

The Sacraments

Sacrament of Baptism

Nothing in creation is the same.
  Indelible the mark, sets one apart,
God crossed ever by the Triune Flame.

Water, oil, priest, to our acclaim,
  And needed for salvation's crucial start,
Nothing in creation is the same.

God's mark upon each soul 'tis His to claim,
  All sin removed, it sanctifies the heart,
God crossed ever by the Triune Flame.

Allows God's grace to enter, and inflame,
  A new beginning, ever to restart,
Nothing in creation is the same.

Virtues flow within, Creator's aim,
  Christ's Passion, Resurrection to impart,
God crossed ever by the Triune Flame.

If we reject, we have ourselves to blame,
  God, of His own, from us, would not depart,
Nothing in creation is the same.
  God crossed ever by the Triune Flame.

Sacrament of Confirmation

Baptism gives to us a need to know,
  Of the hereafter, and eternity,
Truth to ponder on our journey's throe,
  Amid absurdity, uncertainty.

Adults, when entering, may spend a year,
  Studying the church, that realm of faith,
The Holy Spirit shapes, and we adhere
  An everlasting fount of truth, our swaith.

Infants to be baptized have a wait,
  To be invested with their reasoning.
Age six the usual time, they to relate,
  Years of study, proper seasoning.

Sacramental confirmation holds,
Our destiny, as earthly life unfolds.

Sacrament of the Eucharist

This is My body, said, He broke the bread,
  The wine, this is My blood, He then extolled.
One will betray Me, they then were foretold,
  While the betrayer took his leave and fled.
Lord, could it be me? They thought and said,
  Betray? Who would do this? Some few were polled.
The meal then went on God's manifold,
  None knew that by next day He would be dead.

They ran and scattered as the mob approached.
  Death, then resurrection, as foreseen
He then returned and gathered His small band.
  Amazed! He showed His wounds, and then instilled,
This new covenant, they were between,
  Do this in memory, was His stark command.

Ode to the Sacrament of Reconciliation

We were washed, and brought to sanctity,
  When in baptism we were ransomed free.
But sin reenters, changes radically,
  And we retreat from God, from Him we flee,
As we explore the different ways to live.
  Sinfulness abounds, then takes ourselves.
    We become its slave,
      Are less alive.
Do we continue adding to our selves,
  This burden sin extends unto the grave?

There is a different route for us to go,
  To recognize foul sin for what it brings,
A danger to our souls, and then to know,
  We cannot rid ourselves, there hope begins.
We need to search elsewhere, for help we need,
  And know we cannot do this on our own,
    But where to look?
    And what to heed?
We need be serious in all we're shown,
  But not waylaid because we were mistook.

The church, our fount of truth, in sacred ways,
  Gives us a sacrament of grace to share.
Reconciliation ours to praise,
  This gift from God there's nothing to compare.
Confessing to a priest our sins, sincere,
  And asking God's forgiveness, our free choice.
    Forgiven, we are blessed.
    To God we then adhere.
Grace and peace, a flood, as God's own voice,
  We leave, enhanced, again, our souls at rest.

Sacrament of the Anointing of the Sick

Illness carries with it certain pangs,
  Closure, anguish, suffering, and despair.
While danger lurks from evil's claws and fangs.
  The aged, approaching death, do also share.

As end of life draws near, a shortened length,
  A soul may turn in pain away from God,
The church provides this sacrament for strength,
  As solace for the journey, the beyond.

The priest anoints the forehead and the hands,
  And offers special prayers to obtain grace.
In union with Christ's passion the sick one stands,
  To find the Holy Spirit's warm embrace.

This sacrament for aged and the ill,
The church seeks peace and comfort to fulfill.

Sacrament of Holy Orders

What on earth does holy orders mean?
  From earth alone, discernment does not tell.
Go beyond, the realm where angels dwell,
  To find, what here on earth, we might demean.
Jesus, Son of God, on earth did glean,
  His church, a structure meant to save from hell,
Holy, apostolic, catholic, one, does well,
  To serve until the end times do convene.

Bishops, priests, and deacons were prescribed ,
  To be the clergy of the church so vast.
Sacramental holy orders then,
  A sacred power, the Holy Spirit inscribed.
Consecrated, they serve mankind, and cast,
  Their sacramental blessings, their amen.

Ode to the Sacrament of Matrimony

Contentiousness, the bane of human life.
  Two united find their peace displaced,
When anger, petulance or grief bring strife.
  Disruption two before had never faced.
When married such distress may cause unrest,
  And leave the marriage damaged, on the shoals,
    With separation and divorce,
      Chaos for those so stressed.
Disruption for each member's unmet goals.
  For parents and their children's shaken course.

The church the vehicle of Christ on earth,
  Provides a sacrament for two who wed.
Matrimony, the bride and groom themselves give birth,
  The priest but overseer in their stead.
When two baptized, they then must freely choose,
  This covenant between themselves and God.
    This indispensable plank,
      This bond, this fuse.
God gives grace, their marriage will be shod.
  Lasting sanctity, their God to thank.

Happy they live, happily ever after,
  Yet troubles brew to spoil this fairy tale,
Before they wed both parties should deter,
  And find what causes marriages to fail.
Live chaste, both boy and girl, before they wed.
  Be fully versed in what the church imparts.
    And know "I do" is to begin.
      And each to each embed.
No going back, rejoice, two happy hearts,
  Will carry joy and goodness from within.

28362193R00085

Made in the USA
Columbia, SC
15 October 2018